My Baby Jesus Book of NUMBERS

Books in this Series

My Adam and Eve Book of Opposites
My Noah's Ark Book of Colors
My Baby Jesus Book of Numbers
My Bible Story Book of ABC's

Copyright © 1995 by Educational Publishing Concepts, Inc., Wheaton, Illinois

Published by Concordia Publishing House
3558 S. Jefferson Avenue, St. Louis, MO 63118-3968
Manufactured in the United States of America

1 2 3 4 5 6 7 8 9 10   04 03 02 01 00 99 98 97 96 95

My Baby Jesus Book of NUMBERS

Glenda Palmer

Illustrated by
Rick Incrocci

CPH™
SAINT LOUIS

Why is Christmas the very best birthday of the year? Because it's the birthday of the **1 one** and only baby Jesus, that's why!

Jesus slept in **1 one** manger, filled with hay to make it soft. God placed **1 one** special, sparkling star in the sky above His Son for a night-light.

2 two people, Mary and Joseph, loved and cared for baby Jesus.

Count **2 two** donkeys braying,
2 two cows mooing,
and **2 two** doves cooing.

Wise Men from far away saw Jesus' special star in the sky. They hopped on their camels to find Him. They brought **3 three** birthday presents for Jesus.

Count **4 four** shepherd boys and **4 four** baa-ing sheep. The shepherds looked up in the sky. They heard an angel say, "Jesus is born!"

I can count **5 five** people in my family—my dad, my mom, my brother, my sister, and me. How many people are in your family?

We celebrate the birth of Jesus with a birthday party.
We hold **5 five** chocolate cupcakes.
We blow out **5 five** red candles.
Whoo-oo-oosh!

We make **6 six** shiny Christmas
cards. We draw **6 six** pictures of
baby Jesus.

We sing **7 seven** Christmas carols from **7 seven** songbooks with **7 seven** green covers.

We tie **8 eight** shining angels, blowing **8 eight** golden horns, to **8 eight** branches on the Christmas tree.

My family wraps **9 nine** presents with **9 nine** pieces of green paper. We tie them tight with **9 nine** red ribbons.

10 ten bright Christmas lights and
10 ten twinkling stars shine from
the Christmas tree.

They remind us of the big, sparkling star and the gift God gave us for Christmas— the gift of His **1 one** and only Son to save us from our sin.

We hold hands and say, "Thank You, God, for baby Jesus!"